The Marketplace of Selves

On identity, attention, and survival

By: Trent Goodbaudy

Copyright © 2026 Trent Goodbaudy
All rights reserved.
ISBN: 9798243204057

Trent Goodbaudy

TABLE OF CONTENTS

TABLE OF CONTENTS v
SECTION I — HOW THE MARKET WORKS 1
    Chapter 1 — Who Gets Paid to Speak 3
    Chapter 2 — Metrics as Gravity 11
    Chapter 3 — Advertiser-Friendly Reality 17
SECTION II — THE SHIFT 25
    Chapter 4 — When Expression Becomes Labor 27
    Chapter 5 — The Training No One Notices 35
SECTION III — WHAT IT DOES TO PEOPLE 41
    Chapter 6 — The Split 43
    Chapter 7 — Praise Replaces Truth 51
    Chapter 8 — Performing Even When Alone 59
    Chapter 9 — Survival Without Villains 67
    Chapter 10 — The Cost Question 73
PART IV — TIME 81
    Chapter 11 — Finite 83
    Chapter 12 — This Book Stops Here 91
About the Author 99
About LibertyTruth.org 101

SECTION I — HOW THE MARKET WORKS

Trent Goodbaudy

Chapter 1 — Who Gets Paid to Speak

Not everyone who speaks gets heard.
And not everyone who is heard is allowed to continue.

This isn't new in principle. Power has always shaped which voices travel. What's new is how quietly that power now operates—and how often it looks like neutrality.

Today, speech doesn't disappear because it is illegal or offensive. It disappears because it doesn't meet the conditions required to remain visible.

Those conditions are rarely stated plainly. They don't arrive as rules. They show up as thresholds, scores, flags, and friendliness ratings. Numbers decide what spreads. Filters decide what stays. Permission is granted indirectly, through performance.

At first, this feels fair. Objective, even.
Who could argue with numbers?

But numbers don't just measure behavior. They **shape it**.

Visibility is no longer a byproduct of expression. It is a reward for alignment.

Most people encounter this system innocently. They share something they care about. They watch how it performs. They adjust—not because they were told to, but because the response taught them what survives.

Over time, a pattern forms.

Certain tones travel farther.
Certain emotions linger longer.
Certain truths stall.

No one says, *Don't speak that way.*
The system doesn't need to.

Silence teaches faster than instruction.

INSIDER SIGNAL

You learn what "works" before anyone explains it.
Which words travel.
Which emotions survive.
Which truths cost too much to say out loud.

No one calls it training.
You just stop reaching for the things that disappear you.

Monetization makes this process visible, but it doesn't create it. Payment is simply the moment when alignment becomes explicit.

Before anyone gets paid to speak, they learn **how** to speak.

They learn:

- How long to hold attention
- How often to respond
- How to phrase discomfort so it doesn't unsettle
- How to sound sincere without sounding unstable

These aren't moral lessons. They're survival cues.

When income enters the picture, the lesson hardens.

Speech becomes labor.

And labor, by definition, is evaluated.

The important thing to understand is this:
Getting paid is not the beginning of performance.

It's the confirmation that performance has already been learned.

By the time someone qualifies for visibility-based income, they have usually absorbed the system's preferences deeply enough that they no longer experience them as external pressure. They experience them as instinct.

They don't feel censored.
They feel *skilled*.

That's what makes this difficult to notice.

People often imagine gatekeeping as something dramatic. A rejection. A ban. A clear denial.

What actually happens is softer.

Reach narrows.
Exposure flattens.
Momentum fades.

The message isn't *You can't speak.*
It's *This won't go anywhere.*

And that message changes behavior.

INSIDER SIGNAL

You don't post what you think.
You post what will stay visible.

Over time, the difference stops feeling important.
That's how you know the system worked.

Once visibility is conditional, expression adapts.

People don't stop being honest.
They become selective about *which* honesty appears.

This is where confusion sets in.

Because from the outside, everything still looks real.

The words are sincere.
The tone is warm.
The stories are true.

What's missing isn't honesty—it's **range**.

Certain emotions vanish quietly.
Certain questions stop appearing.
Certain conflicts resolve too cleanly.

The world doesn't get quieter.
It gets narrower.

Advertiser-friendly language didn't invent this narrowing. It simply made it legible.

When expression must remain compatible with approval, complexity becomes risky. Ambivalence becomes suspicious. Anger becomes inconvenient. Grief becomes something to soften, reframe, or resolve quickly.

Not because these emotions are wrong—but because they are unpredictable.

And unpredictability doesn't monetize well.

This creates a strange outcome.

The most visible voices often sound calm, certain, and agreeable—not because they feel that way, but because those qualities keep them present in the system.

The system doesn't reward truth.
It rewards **stability**.

And stability, in this context, means not disrupting the flow.

INSIDER SIGNAL

You know which emotions are safe to show.
You learned them without being taught.
You can't remember when you learned the others weren't.

It's important to say this clearly:
There is nothing inherently wrong with being paid to speak.

People have always earned a living through communication. Teaching, storytelling, persuasion, and performance are ancient forms of work.

The difference now is **who decides what counts as acceptable expression**—and how early that decision enters the process.

When speech is filtered before it's fully formed, people don't lose their voice. They lose contact with parts of it.

This doesn't feel like oppression.
It feels like professionalism.

Most participants in this system are not trying to deceive anyone. They are adapting. They are learning how to remain visible, relevant, and solvent.

That matters.

Because blame obscures the real issue.

The problem is not that people perform.
The problem is that performance is increasingly **required before expression is allowed to exist**.

When speaking freely becomes optional—and speaking acceptably becomes necessary—people reorganize themselves accordingly.

Quietly.
Reasonably.
Without complaint.

By the time someone notices the cost, it often feels too late to name.

They've built an audience.
They've found a rhythm.
They've learned what to avoid.

Nothing dramatic happened.

They just stopped reaching for certain thoughts.

This chapter isn't here to accuse anyone.

It's here to clarify the conditions.

Because once you see how permission operates, you can begin to notice what happens inside when speech becomes something you earn rather than something you offer.

That noticing is where the rest of this book begins.

Chapter 2 — Metrics as Gravity

Metrics don't give orders.
They don't tell anyone what to do.

They don't need to.

Numbers work the way gravity does. Quietly. Constantly. Without asking permission.

No one wakes up intending to change how they speak because of metrics. They change because numbers make certain outcomes feel heavier than others. Some choices rise. Others sink. Over time, movement adjusts.

Not through force.
Through repetition.

At first, metrics feel helpful. Clean. Informational.

They appear to answer simple questions:

- Did this reach anyone?
- Did it land?
- Was it worth repeating?

The numbers seem neutral. Honest. They don't judge—so it feels safe to trust them.

But neutrality is an illusion.

Metrics don't measure meaning.
They measure response.

And response is not the same thing.

What metrics really track is **reaction speed**.

They reward what:

- Grabs attention quickly
- Holds it just long enough
- Produces a visible response

They don't ask whether something was true, careful, or accurate.
They ask whether it moved.

Over time, this distinction matters.

Because people don't change their values.
They change their **timing**.

INSIDER SIGNAL

You don't feel pressured.
You feel informed.

That's how pressure gets inside without being named.

The strange thing about metrics is that they don't feel like control.
They feel like feedback.

And feedback feels reasonable.

If something performs well, you're inclined to repeat it.
If something falls flat, you pause.

This isn't manipulation.
It's learning.

But learning has direction.

And when the environment consistently rewards one direction, behavior follows—even without intent.

People often say, "I don't care about the numbers."

And they're usually telling the truth.

What they care about is **whether what they said mattered**.

Metrics step into that gap.

They quietly redefine what "mattered" means.

Over time, anticipation replaces reflection.

Before speaking, people begin to sense:

- How this will land
- Who it will reach
- Whether it will stall

This happens quickly. Often before a thought is fully formed.

Not because people are calculating—but because they've been trained.

INSIDER SIGNAL

You know the response before you post.
You can feel it in advance.
That feeling starts guiding the choice.

This is where metrics stop being external.

They move inside.

People begin to self-adjust before the numbers arrive. They soften language. They sharpen phrasing. They remove edges that slow momentum.

Not because they were told to—but because experience taught them what keeps things moving.

The result is subtle.

Expression becomes **predictive** instead of exploratory.

Predictive expression doesn't ask, *Is this accurate?*
It asks, *Will this work?*

That shift doesn't feel dangerous. It feels efficient.

But efficiency has a cost.

Exploration allows uncertainty.
Prediction avoids it.

And when uncertainty disappears, so does range.

The most important effect of metrics isn't what they reward.

It's what they **discourage quietly**.

Nuance slows things down.
Ambivalence confuses response.
Complexity resists compression.

None of these are punished.
They're simply ignored.

And being ignored feels heavier than being corrected.

INSIDER SIGNAL

You hesitate, not because something is wrong,
but because it might not move.

That hesitation starts making decisions for you.

When metrics shape behavior long enough, people stop noticing the shaping.

They begin to believe their adjusted expression is just maturity. Professionalism. Growth.

And sometimes it is.

But sometimes it's something else.

Sometimes it's the gradual replacement of internal judgment with external confirmation.

This doesn't happen because people are weak.

It happens because humans are responsive.

We adapt to environments.
We learn what keeps us included.
We notice what gets reinforced.

Metrics exploit that responsiveness without ever announcing themselves as authority.

Gravity doesn't need to be explained to work.

Metrics don't either.

They simply exist—and over time, everything learns how to move in relation to them.

This is the moment where the system stops feeling like something *around* you and starts feeling like something *within* you.

And once that happens, the question is no longer about numbers.

It's about **who you're listening to when you decide what to say**.

That question doesn't require an answer yet.

It only requires noticing.

That noticing is where the internal turn begins.

Chapter 3 — Advertiser-Friendly Reality

Not all emotions travel equally.

Some move easily.
Others stall.
A few disappear entirely.

This isn't because anyone decided they were wrong. It's because some emotions are predictable—and others aren't.

In systems built around attention, predictability matters.

"Advertiser-friendly" sounds technical. Neutral. Practical.

But what it really means is **emotionally manageable**.

Language that doesn't spike uncertainty.
Stories that don't linger too long in discomfort.
Expression that resolves cleanly.

Nothing too sharp.
Nothing too unsettled.
Nothing that makes people leave the room.

At first, this filtering feels reasonable.

Of course platforms want stability.
Of course brands avoid risk.
Of course chaos isn't profitable.

No one argues with that.

The problem isn't the intention.
It's the side effect.

Certain emotions become easier to show:

- Inspiration
- Gratitude
- Mild frustration
- Hope framed as progress

They fit well. They move smoothly. They keep attention flowing.

Other emotions begin to fade:

- Anger that doesn't resolve
- Grief that doesn't uplift
- Confusion without clarity
- Doubt without a lesson

These emotions don't disappear because they're untrue.
They disappear because they don't compress well.

INSIDER SIGNAL

You notice which feelings land.
You notice which ones slow things down.
Over time, you stop offering the second kind.

This is how "safe" expression becomes default expression.

Not because people are hiding—but because they're adapting.

They learn which tones keep conversations open.
Which moods sustain reach.
Which stories invite continuation.

They aren't censoring themselves consciously.

They're editing instinctively.

Neutrality plays a special role here.

Neutral language doesn't provoke.
It doesn't alarm.
It doesn't demand a response.

That makes it valuable.

Neutrality travels far because it doesn't create friction. It allows everyone to agree—or disengage—without cost.

In an attention economy, low friction is currency.

But neutrality has limits.

When neutrality becomes the safest option, it starts replacing precision.

Instead of saying what's accurate, people say what's acceptable.

Instead of naming conflict, they smooth it.

Instead of staying with discomfort, they resolve it early.

Not to deceive—but to remain compatible.

INSIDER SIGNAL

You soften something true
so it won't cause problems.

You tell yourself you're being considerate.

This creates a strange emotional landscape.

Everything sounds reasonable.
Everything feels calm.
Everything appears measured.

But underneath, something is missing.

Range.

Not everyone is angry.
Not everyone is grieving.
Not everyone is confused.

But *someone always is*.

When those emotions stop appearing, it doesn't mean they stopped existing.

It means they stopped being shown.

Over time, people begin to internalize the filter.

They don't wait to see what's allowed.
They already know.

Before speaking, they ask—quietly:

- Will this sound unstable?
- Will this make things uncomfortable?
- Will this stall momentum?

And if the answer feels uncertain, the expression adjusts.

INSIDER SIGNAL

You rehearse a cleaner version of what you feel.
The messier one stays private.
Eventually, even you stop visiting it.

This isn't oppression.

It's accommodation.

People don't feel silenced.
They feel *professional*.

They learn how to stay inside the lines without noticing where the lines came from.

That's why this process doesn't feel hostile.

It feels like growth.

The danger isn't that truth disappears.

It's that truth becomes **conditional**.

Allowed only when:

- It's calm enough
- It's brief enough
- It resolves quickly enough
- It doesn't disrupt the environment it appears in

Truth that takes time stops appearing.

Truth that unsettles stops traveling.

This is how emotional filtering works without villains.

No one enforces it directly.
No one needs to.

The incentives do the work.

And the longer this environment persists, the more people forget that expression once included the full range of what it meant to be human.

By the time someone notices the narrowing, it doesn't feel like loss.

It feels like restraint.
Maturity.
Self-control.

But restraint isn't the same as accuracy.

And self-control isn't the same as self-contact.

This chapter isn't asking for louder emotion.

It's asking for **honest range**.

Because when only certain emotions are allowed to appear, people don't just change what they show.

They change what they notice in themselves.

That quiet shift is where self-censorship begins—not as a rule, but as a habit.

And habits don't announce themselves.

They just start deciding what feels sayable.

Trent Goodbaudy

SECTION II — THE SHIFT

Trent Goodbaudy

Chapter 4 — When Expression Becomes Labor

Expression doesn't change all at once.
It changes in increments.

At first, speaking feels natural. You say something because it's present. Because it wants to be said. There's no urgency to shape it. No pressure to deliver it cleanly.

Then the environment shifts.

Response becomes visible.
Timing becomes noticeable.
Format begins to matter.

Expression slows down—not because thought deepens, but because outcome enters the room.

Labor is defined by output.

It asks:

- Can this be repeated?
- Can this be scheduled?
- Can this be measured?
- Can this be evaluated?

When expression enters a system built on output, it starts answering those questions—even if no one asks them directly.

Speaking slowly becomes posting deliberately.
Sharing becomes releasing.
Thought becomes content.

Nothing dramatic changes.
Everything just becomes *usable*.

INSIDER SIGNAL

You don't just say things anymore.
You package them.

That shift feels small—until it doesn't.

Once expression is expected to perform, people begin thinking in containers.

They don't notice it happening.
They just feel it guiding them.

Is this a post or a comment?
Is this a clip or a story?
Is this long-form or short?
Is this worth saving for later?

The thought arrives already shaped.

This is where spontaneity thins.

Spontaneity doesn't disappear because people stop caring.
It disappears because it becomes inefficient.

Unstructured expression doesn't scale well.
It doesn't schedule cleanly.
It doesn't guarantee response.

So it gets postponed.

"I'll share this later."
"I'll clean this up."
"I'll make this clearer."

Eventually, later never comes.

INSIDER SIGNAL

You feel something real,
but you wait for the right format.

The feeling passes before the format arrives.

When expression becomes labor, it starts borrowing rules from work.

Consistency matters.
Tone matters.
Reliability matters.

These aren't bad values.

But they aren't neutral either.

They privilege what can be repeated over what needs to be said once.
They favor what fits over what interrupts.
They reward clarity—even when clarity hasn't arrived yet.

This is the moment where people stop discovering what they think by speaking—and start speaking only what they already know how to deliver.

Exploration turns into execution.

And execution has a cost.

People often confuse this shift with growth.

They say they're more intentional now.
More careful.
More strategic.

Sometimes that's true.

But sometimes it's something else.

Sometimes it's the moment when expression stops being a place where truth forms—and becomes a place where truth is *filtered*.

INSIDER SIGNAL

You don't use expression to find out what you think anymore.
You use it to confirm what will work.

That's when it starts feeling heavy.

Labor requires stamina.

So expression begins conserving energy.

People reuse phrases.
They repeat structures.
They stick with what's familiar.

This isn't laziness.
It's adaptation.

But adaptation always trades one thing for another.

What's gained is efficiency.
What's lost is freshness.

When expression was spontaneous, it surprised the speaker as much as the listener.

When expression becomes labor, surprise becomes a liability.

Unpredictability risks misunderstanding.
Misunderstanding risks disengagement.
Disengagement risks disappearance.

So expression tightens.

This is the core transformation of the marketplace of selves.

Not that people lie.
Not that people perform.

But that **expression stops being a living process and becomes a managed output**.

Once that happens, people don't feel censored.

They feel tired.

The exhaustion doesn't come from speaking too much.
It comes from speaking *after* translation.

Every thought passes through:

- Will this land?
- Will this fit?
- Will this move?

By the time it reaches the surface, it's already been worked.

INSIDER SIGNAL

You finish saying something
and feel relief instead of clarity.

That relief tells you it was work.

This chapter isn't suggesting that labor is wrong.

Work has always been part of human life.

What's new is how often people now **work before they speak**, rather than speak and discover what matters.

When expression requires preparation, permission, and positioning, something fundamental changes.

The voice doesn't vanish.

It just stops being the place where contact happens.

This is the center of the book because everything else follows from here.

Once expression becomes labor:

- Metrics gain influence
- Safety narrows range
- Performance replaces presence

And once that happens, the most important questions move inward.

Not:
How do I say this better?

But:
Who am I speaking from now?

That question doesn't need to be answered yet.

It only needs to be noticed.

From here on, the book turns toward what that change does to people—not as creators, but as humans.

Chapter 5 — The Training No One Notices

Most training announces itself.

There are instructions.
Examples.
Corrections.

This kind doesn't.

No one sits you down and explains how to survive inside visibility systems. No handbook arrives. No authority figure lays out the rules.

You learn by watching what continues—and what fades.

At first, it feels like simple observation.

You notice which posts travel farther.
Which tones invite replies.
Which ideas stall quietly.

You adjust, not out of fear, but out of curiosity.

What works?

That question feels harmless.

This is why the process doesn't feel like control.

Control feels external.
This feels internal.

It feels like learning the room.
Like reading social cues.
Like becoming more skilled.

And skill is usually a good thing.

INSIDER SIGNAL

No one tells you to change.
You just remember what happened last time.

That memory starts guiding you.

Conditioning works best when it doesn't feel imposed.

If someone demanded compliance, resistance would appear.
If someone enforced rules, people would push back.

Instead, the environment teaches through consequence.

Not punishment.
Just outcome.

Things that align continue.
Things that don't quietly stop.

Over time, the lesson sticks.

People often misunderstand conditioning as manipulation.

It isn't.

It's responsiveness.

Humans are good at adapting. We always have been. We adjust to weather, culture, danger, opportunity. This is one of our strengths.

The problem isn't adaptation.

It's **what adaptation replaces**.

When people say, "I've grown," they're often right.

They're calmer.
More measured.
Less reactive.

But growth and compression can look similar from the outside.

Both reduce volatility.
Both smooth edges.
Both create stability.

Only one preserves range.

INSIDER SIGNAL

You tell yourself you're being more mature.
You don't mention what you stopped saying to get there.

Adaptation feels like maturity because it reduces friction.

You learn how not to upset people.
How not to derail conversations.
How not to complicate things.

This makes life easier.

It also makes expression narrower.

But because the narrowing happens gradually, it rarely registers as loss.

It registers as refinement.

The training works because it's cumulative.

One adjustment doesn't matter.
Neither does the next.

But eventually, expression arrives pre-edited.

Not because someone demanded it—but because the system made the alternative inefficient.

What makes this process difficult to see is that it rewards good intentions.

People aren't trying to deceive.
They're trying to connect.
They're trying to be understood.
They're trying to stay included.

Those are reasonable goals.

So the training hides inside them.

INSIDER SIGNAL

You learn how to stay welcome.
You don't notice when that becomes the priority.

Blame doesn't help here.

There's no villain to confront.
No authority to overthrow.

The system doesn't need enforcement because people internalize the lesson themselves.

That's why anger misses the point.

And that's why compassion matters.

Most people don't realize they've been trained until something unexpected slips out.

A sentence that feels too sharp.
An emotion that doesn't resolve.
A thought that doesn't fit the rhythm.

The discomfort isn't just social.

It's internal.

They feel exposed.

That exposure is revealing.

It shows how far adaptation has gone—not as betrayal, but as habit.

And habits don't form because people are weak.

They form because they work.

This chapter exists to remove blame.

Not to excuse everything—but to clarify the process.

Because once people understand that conditioning happened quietly, without orders or force, they can stop accusing themselves for adapting.

They can also start noticing **what adaptation cost them**.

Training that announces itself can be questioned.

Training that feels like maturity usually isn't.

That's why noticing it matters.

Not so it can be undone—but so it stops operating invisibly.

From here on, the book turns toward what happens inside once this training has been absorbed.

Not how to escape it.

Just how to see it clearly.

SECTION III — WHAT IT DOES TO PEOPLE

Trent Goodbaudy

Chapter 6 — The Split

The split doesn't arrive suddenly.

There's no moment where a person decides to become two things. No conscious choice to separate who they are from how they appear.

It happens gradually, as adaptation accumulates.

At first, there's just a slight adjustment. A tone shift. A preference for certain words. A way of presenting that feels easier to manage.

Then one day, something feels off.

Not wrong.
Just thinner.

Persona is not deception.

Persona is the version of the self that functions in a specific environment. Everyone has one. Work personas. Social personas. Public-facing selves.

Persona becomes a problem only when it **replaces presence**.

Presence is what you feel like when you are not managing how you appear. When attention is inward. When expression is unfiltered by outcome.

The split happens when those two drift too far apart.

INSIDER SIGNAL

You sound like yourself.
But you don't feel like yourself.

That difference starts costing energy.

Public self and private self begin to operate on different rules.

Public self asks:

- Is this appropriate?
- Is this acceptable?
- Will this land?

Private self asks:

- Is this accurate?
- Is this honest?
- Does this matter?

When those questions no longer overlap, tension builds.

The strange thing is that this tension often increases when things are going well.

Visibility rises.
Engagement improves.
Opportunities expand.

From the outside, everything looks aligned.

From the inside, something tightens.

People expect success to feel energizing.

But success inside performance systems often feels heavy.

Because the more effective the persona becomes, the more carefully it must be maintained.

Consistency becomes a requirement.
Deviation becomes risky.

The public self hardens into a shape that works.

INSIDER SIGNAL

You feel relief when a performance ends.
Not because it was hard—
but because you can stop being managed.

This is why exhaustion doesn't always come from overwork.

It comes from **monitoring**.

Monitoring tone.
Monitoring response.
Monitoring perception.

Even rest becomes strategic.

People don't just rest.
They recover.

Recovery implies depletion.

The split deepens when people start identifying with their persona.

They say, "This is just who I am now."

Sometimes that's true.

But sometimes it's simply the version that survived.

The private self doesn't disappear.
It goes quiet.

When the private self stays quiet too long, people lose access to internal feedback.

They know how they appear.
They're less sure how they feel.

They can sense approval.
They struggle to sense alignment.

This is where confusion sets in.

INSIDER SIGNAL

You check how something was received
before you check how you feel about it.

That order matters.

Fragmentation doesn't feel dramatic.

It feels functional.

Life keeps moving. Responsibilities are met. People respond positively.

But inside, expression stops being a place of discovery.

It becomes a place of maintenance.

The cost of the split isn't always obvious.

Sometimes it shows up as fatigue that sleep doesn't fix.
Sometimes as irritability without a clear cause.
Sometimes as numbness where enthusiasm used to be.

People often blame themselves.

They assume they're ungrateful.
Burned out.
Unmotivated.

But the issue isn't effort.

It's division.

Being split requires constant negotiation.

What can be shown.
What must be withheld.
What needs translation.

That negotiation consumes attention.

And attention is finite.

This chapter isn't about choosing between public and private selves.

Persona is not the enemy.

The problem is when presence no longer has a place to operate.

When every expression is filtered through how it will be received, the internal world loses oxygen.

The exhaustion people feel—even when things are "working"—is often the body's response to this loss of contact.

Not a failure.
Not weakness.

A signal.

From here, the book moves deeper into what replaces internal contact when persona dominates—and how praise, agreement, and performance step in to fill the gap.

But first, the split has to be seen.

Because once it's visible, it's no longer total.

And that alone changes something.

Chapter 7 — Praise Replaces Truth

Praise feels good for a reason.

It signals safety.
Belonging.
Confirmation that you're aligned with the environment around you.

There's nothing wrong with that.

But when praise becomes the primary form of feedback, something subtle shifts.

Truth stops being the reference point.
Response takes its place.

Agreement feels safer than honesty because agreement doesn't ask for correction.

It doesn't slow things down.
It doesn't create tension.
It doesn't risk misunderstanding.

Agreement keeps momentum.

And in systems where momentum equals visibility, safety starts to look like wisdom.

At first, feedback feels helpful.

Likes.
Positive comments.
Affirming messages.

They seem to answer an important question: *Did this land?*

But over time, feedback stops being descriptive and starts becoming **directive**.

Not because anyone intends it that way—but because repetition teaches.

What's praised returns.
What isn't fades.

INSIDER SIGNAL

You notice what gets affirmed.
You bring more of that next time—
without deciding to.

This is how feedback becomes guidance.

Not through instruction, but through reinforcement.

People don't ask, *Is this true?*
They ask, *Is this received?*

The difference is small at first.

Then it compounds.

Praise simplifies.

It highlights what's agreeable and minimizes what's complex. It rewards clarity even when clarity isn't accurate yet.

Nuanced thoughts don't always get traction.
Unfinished ideas don't travel far.
Questions don't perform as well as conclusions.

So people adjust.

They arrive with answers instead of explorations.

Over time, honesty begins to feel risky—not because it's wrong, but because it's inefficient.

Honest uncertainty slows response.
Honest disagreement disrupts flow.
Honest discomfort complicates things.

None of these are punished.

They're simply less rewarded.

INSIDER SIGNAL

You start editing for agreement.
You call it being thoughtful.

Something else quietly leaves the room.

Silence enters as a strategy.

Not silence born of reflection—but silence born of calculation.

If something won't be received well, it might be better not to say it at all.

This doesn't feel like avoidance.

It feels intelligent.

Silence looks mature because it avoids conflict.

It preserves harmony.
It protects reputation.
It keeps relationships smooth.

But silence chosen for safety isn't neutral.

It teaches the speaker which truths are negotiable.

When praise replaces truth, relationships begin to shift.

People don't argue less because they agree more.

They argue less because disagreement no longer feels worth the cost.

Conversations become pleasant.
They also become thinner.

INSIDER SIGNAL

You hold something back
because it would complicate things.

That restraint starts feeling like wisdom.

Over time, people lose practice telling the truth relationally.

Not dramatic truth.
Not confrontational truth.

Simple truth.

"I don't know."
"I'm unsure."
"That doesn't sit right."
"I'm still thinking."

These statements don't disappear because they're false.

They disappear because they don't resolve cleanly.

Praise fills the gap left behind.

It reassures.
It smooths.
It keeps things moving.

But it doesn't challenge.

And without challenge, relationships stop being places where clarity sharpens.

They become places where alignment is maintained.

This doesn't mean praise is bad.

It means praise is incomplete.

When praise becomes the dominant currency, truth becomes optional.

Optional truths are the first ones to go.

The long-term cost isn't dishonesty.

It's **distance**.

Distance between what's felt and what's said.
Distance between what's known and what's shared.
Distance between people who agree but no longer reveal much to each other.

This chapter isn't calling for more conflict.

It's naming a substitution.

When agreement replaces honesty, relationships don't break.

They stabilize.

And stability, in this context, often means less is at stake.

Silence feels intelligent because it avoids loss.

But loss isn't the only signal worth paying attention to.

From here, the book moves into what happens when performance and agreement no longer require an audience—when they follow people into their private lives.

Because once praise becomes guidance, it doesn't stop at the edge of public interaction.

It keeps going.

Even when no one is watching.

Chapter 8 — Performing Even When Alone

The most effective systems don't require supervision.

Once the rules are internalized, enforcement becomes unnecessary.

This is the stage most people don't recognize—because nothing external is happening anymore.

No metrics.
No feedback.
No audience.

And yet, performance continues.

People rehearse posts they never publish.

They shape sentences in their head.
They refine phrasing.
They imagine responses.

Sometimes they do this intentionally.
Often they don't.

The thought arrives already arranged, already prepared for an audience that isn't there.

INSIDER SIGNAL

You finish composing something in your head.
You never intended to share it.
It still went through the same filter.

This is where the market moves inside.

Expression no longer waits for permission.
It preemptively adapts.

Internal narration changes tone.

Thoughts become cleaner.
Edges soften.
Conclusions arrive faster.

Not because the mind prefers it—but because the environment trained it.

People often believe internal freedom is automatic.

That whatever happens privately is untouched.

But habits don't respect boundaries.

If expression is filtered long enough on the outside, the filter becomes the default setting.

Inner speech begins to sound like outer speech.

Careful.
Measured.
Optimized.

People don't notice this as loss.

They notice it as coherence.

INSIDER SIGNAL

Your private thoughts sound presentable.
You don't remember deciding that mattered.

When the market moves inside, spontaneity becomes rare.

Even alone, people feel the urge to resolve thoughts quickly. To land somewhere. To avoid uncertainty.

Ambivalence feels inefficient.
Confusion feels unfinished.
Open-endedness feels wasteful.

So the mind closes loops early.

This creates a strange contradiction.

People have more time alone than ever.
But less internal quiet.

Thoughts don't wander as freely.
They organize themselves.

Not around truth—but around clarity.

Clarity feels good.

It reduces tension.
It creates a sense of control.

But clarity reached too early replaces understanding with conclusion.

And conclusions end exploration.

The system no longer needs to correct people.

They correct themselves.

They notice which thoughts feel sharable.
They favor those.

They notice which thoughts feel awkward.
They abandon them.

No one told them to.

The training already did its work.

INSIDER SIGNAL

You abandon a thought
because it doesn't sound right yet.

You don't give it time to become right.

This is where performance stops being social and becomes cognitive.

It shapes not just what people say—but how they think.

Thoughts that don't resolve cleanly stop being pursued.
Questions without answers stop being held.
Contradictions stop being tolerated.

Not because they're false—but because they don't fit the rhythm.

When enforcement disappears, people often assume freedom has returned.

But freedom isn't just the absence of rules.

It's the presence of **unfiltered attention**.

When attention remains organized around how something would be received—even in private—the market is still operating.

Just invisibly.

This doesn't mean people are trapped.

It means they're efficient.

And efficiency, left unchecked, replaces curiosity.

The cost of internal performance isn't immediate.

It accumulates.

People feel restless without knowing why.
They feel busy without doing much.
They feel tired without exertion.

They call it mental fatigue.

But what's often happening is constant, unnecessary self-management.

When the market moves inside, people don't need surveillance.

They've become fluent in self-adjustment.

That fluency feels normal.

Until one day, a thought arrives that doesn't know how to behave.

It feels awkward.
Unpolished.
Incomplete.

People often dismiss it.

But that thought is important.

Because it hasn't learned the rules yet.

This chapter isn't asking you to trust every thought.

It's asking you to notice **which ones never get airtime anymore**—even internally.

Because once expression is managed at the level of thought, the system no longer needs power.

It has habit.

And habit is quieter than control.

From here, the book turns toward responsibility—not blame, not guilt—but the human cost of adapting so well that nothing pushes back anymore.

That's where the next question begins.

Chapter 9 — Survival Without Villains

It's tempting to look for someone to blame.

A platform.
An algorithm.
A corporation.
A culture.

Blame gives shape to discomfort. It offers a target. It creates a sense of moral clarity.

But blame doesn't explain what's actually happening.

Because most people aren't performing out of vanity.

They're performing to survive.

People perform to eat.
They perform to belong.
They perform to remain visible enough not to disappear.

These are not shallow motives.
They're human ones.

Visibility now overlaps with opportunity. Opportunity overlaps with income. Income overlaps with safety.

That changes behavior.

Not because people are corrupt—but because they're responsive.

This is why villains don't fit the story.

There is no single decision-maker shaping every outcome. No centralized intent enforcing conformity.

What exists instead is a set of incentives that quietly reward certain adaptations and ignore others.

People follow what works.

That doesn't make them dishonest.
It makes them practical.

INSIDER SIGNAL

You don't feel like you're selling out.
You feel like you're being realistic.

That distinction matters.

Resentment often enters when people sense loss without understanding cause.

They feel constrained.
They feel flattened.
They feel tired.

So they look outward.

But resentment aimed at individuals misses the point.

Most people inside these systems are doing the best they can with the conditions they're given.

They aren't trying to manipulate anyone.
They aren't trying to erase truth.

They're trying to stay afloat.

Survival pressures don't announce themselves as pressure.

They feel like responsibility.

Pay bills.
Meet expectations.
Maintain relevance.
Stay employable.

These are reasonable concerns.

They also shape expression more effectively than force ever could.

INSIDER SIGNAL

You justify the adjustment
because the alternative feels irresponsible.

That logic is hard to argue with.

When people adapt for survival, they rarely experience it as compromise.

They experience it as adulthood.

They learn to be careful.
They learn to be strategic.
They learn to avoid unnecessary risk.

In many contexts, this is wisdom.

The trouble begins when survival logic extends beyond necessity and starts governing identity.

Resentment doesn't help because it assumes bad faith.

But the system doesn't run on bad people.

It runs on good people adapting.

Parents.
Artists.
Teachers.
Creators.
Workers.

People with values.

People with limits.

Blame also creates false distance.

It allows people to say, *I would never do that*, while doing something similar under a different name.

Everyone performs.

The difference isn't between performers and non-performers.

It's between those who notice the cost and those who don't.

INSIDER SIGNAL

You tell yourself you'd be more honest
if things were different.

You don't question when "different" arrives.

Survival systems narrow choice.

They don't remove it—but they weight it.

Some paths feel lighter.
Others feel heavy.

Over time, people stop exploring the heavier ones.

Not because they're wrong—but because they're costly.

Understanding this removes moral superiority.

It also removes despair.

If no one is the villain, then no one needs to be defeated.

What's required instead is clarity.

Clarity doesn't mean withdrawing.

It doesn't mean refusing to participate.

And it doesn't mean pretending survival doesn't matter.

It means recognizing that performance is often a response to conditions—not a reflection of character.

This chapter exists to clear the ground.

To say:
You're not broken for adapting.
You're not shallow for caring about survival.
You're not wrong for wanting to belong.

But adaptation always has a price.

And once that price becomes visible, resentment is no longer useful.

Something else takes its place.

Responsibility.

Not responsibility for fixing the system.

Responsibility for noticing what it asks of you—and what you're willing to give.

That's where the next question begins.

Not about blame.

But about cost.

Chapter 10 — The Cost Question

Performance isn't the problem.

People have always performed.
They've worked, presented, negotiated, adapted.

Performance is how humans survive together.

What matters is **what performance costs**.

The mistake is thinking the issue is effort.

People assume they're tired because they're doing too much.
Because they're overextended. Because they need rest.

Sometimes that's true.

But often, the exhaustion comes from something else.

From **estrangement**.

Estrangement is what happens when what you do requires you to step away from what you feel, notice, or mean.

Not dramatically.
Not all at once.

Just enough to keep going.

There's a difference between spending energy and spending contact.

Energy is renewable.
Contact is not.

You can rest and regain energy.
But when contact is lost—when you stop feeling present while you act—rest doesn't restore it.

That's why some people feel tired even after doing nothing.

INSIDER SIGNAL

You can work hard and feel intact.
You can also feel drained without working much at all.

The difference is contact.

Spending energy looks like effort.

You concentrate.
You exert yourself.
You recover.

Spending contact looks quieter.

You translate.
You adjust.
You hold something back.

You don't feel the cost immediately.

You feel it later—as flatness, distance, or numbness.

This is where ethics quietly enter the picture—not as rules, but as signals.

Ethics here don't mean right and wrong.

They mean **sustainable or unsustainable**.

Work that spends energy can be repeated.
Work that spends contact cannot.

Eventually, something gives.

People often talk about "doing what you love."

That phrase gets dismissed because it sounds idealistic.

But the real issue isn't love.

It's presence.

Doing something you love doesn't mean it's easy.
It doesn't mean it pays well.
It doesn't mean it avoids effort.

It means that while doing it, **you remain inside yourself**.

INSIDER SIGNAL

You can feel effort without resistance.
That's how you know contact is still there.

This distinction explains why two people can do similar work and experience it completely differently.

One feels alive, even when tired.
The other feels hollow, even when successful.

The difference isn't talent or discipline.

It's whether the work requires ongoing self-silencing.

Self-silencing doesn't always look like lying.

Often it looks like:

- Saying less than you notice
- Smoothing what feels sharp
- Resolving feelings early
- Staying neutral when something matters

Each adjustment seems reasonable.

But over time, they accumulate.

INSIDER SIGNAL

You tell yourself it's just how things are.
You don't notice what you stopped bringing with you.

This is why performance itself isn't unethical.

People perform for money.
Everyone does.

The ethical line isn't payment.

It's **whether the work requires you to be absent while doing it**.

When work asks for energy, you can recover.

When it asks for disappearance—even partial disappearance—it creates debt.

Not financial debt.

Internal debt.

Internal debt doesn't show up on schedules.

It shows up as:

- Irritability without cause
- Loss of curiosity
- Difficulty feeling satisfied
- Relief when things stop

People often misinterpret these signs.

They assume they need more success.
More recognition.
More security.

But more of the same rarely fixes a cost that's structural.

This chapter isn't asking anyone to quit.

It isn't asking anyone to rebel.

And it isn't asking anyone to romanticize struggle.

It's asking a simpler question.

What does this cost me—while I'm doing it?

Not later.
Not eventually.

Now.

When people begin asking that question honestly, they don't immediately change their lives.

They change their awareness.

They notice when they're present.
They notice when they're managing.
They notice when effort feels clean—and when it feels hollow.

That noticing is ethical without being moral.

It doesn't judge.

It clarifies.

Performance will always exist.

The question is whether it asks you to spend energy—or to spend yourself.

Once that distinction is visible, something shifts.

Not outwardly.

Inwardly.

And from there, different choices become possible—not because they're demanded, but because contact has returned.

The Marketplace of Selves: *On identity, attention, and survival*

That's the line this book has been slowly drawing.

Not between good and bad.

But between what costs effort—and what costs **you**.

Trent Goodbaudy

PART IV — TIME

Trent Goodbaudy

Chapter 11 — Finite

Time was always limited.

Nothing about this moment made that true.
Nothing about technology changed it.
Nothing about work, visibility, or systems created it.

It was always this way.

What changed is how easy it became to forget.

When life feels open-ended, urgency fades.

Not panic—just presence.

People assume there will be time later. Time to rest. Time to do what matters. Time to return to what feels meaningful once survival is secure.

Later becomes a container for everything postponed.

Postponement rarely feels like denial.

It feels responsible.

"I'll do that once things settle."
"After this phase."

"When I'm more stable."
"When there's room."

There's always a reason.

And the reasons usually make sense.

INSIDER SIGNAL

You don't feel like you're giving something up.
You feel like you're being patient.

Those two aren't always the same.

People postpone gratification not because they don't know what matters.

Most people know.

They postpone because gratification is treated as a reward—something earned after survival is handled.

The problem is that survival keeps expanding.

New responsibilities appear.
New pressures replace old ones.
New versions of "later" take shape.

The finish line moves.

Quietly.

"Later" is persuasive because it sounds generous.

It promises return.
It suggests fairness.
It implies that what matters isn't being denied—just delayed.

But time doesn't store intention.

It only passes.

INSIDER SIGNAL

You assume you'll recognize the right moment.
You don't notice how often that moment slides forward.

Finite time changes the meaning of cost.

When time feels abundant, misalignment feels tolerable.
When time is acknowledged, misalignment becomes visible.

Not dramatic.
Just clearer.

People begin to notice how much of their day requires translation.
How often they adjust instead of arrive.
How rarely they feel present while doing what fills their time.

This isn't about urgency.

Urgency creates pressure.
Pressure creates more performance.

This is about **honesty**.

Honesty about what's being postponed—and why.

People often wait for permission to live meaningfully.

Permission from money.
Permission from stability.
Permission from circumstance.

But permission rarely arrives cleanly.

It arrives as *enough*.

Enough security.
Enough confidence.
Enough time.

Enough never settles.

INSIDER SIGNAL

You tell yourself you're not ready yet.
You don't define what "ready" would mean.

Finite time doesn't demand drastic change.

It doesn't require quitting.
It doesn't insist on transformation.

It simply reframes value.

What costs contact becomes harder to ignore.
What preserves contact becomes easier to recognize.

This is where gratification needs to be understood correctly.

Gratification isn't indulgence.
It isn't escape.
It isn't ease.

Gratification is **alignment felt while doing something**.

It's the sense that effort is connected—not managed.
That time spent is inhabited—not endured.

That feeling doesn't require perfection.

It requires presence.

When people say, "I'll do what gratifies me later," they often mean, "I'll allow myself to feel present later."

But presence isn't a reward.

It's a condition.

And conditions don't wait.

Time being finite doesn't mean life is short.

It means **deferral has consequences**.

Not moral consequences.
Experiential ones.

What's postponed too long stops feeling reachable—not because it vanished, but because the habit of postponing took over.

INSIDER SIGNAL

You notice how long it's been
since you felt fully inside what you were doing.

That realization doesn't shout.
It just sits there.

This chapter isn't asking you to seize the day.

It's asking you to notice the trade.

What's being postponed in exchange for what?
What's being preserved—and what's being spent?

Finite time sharpens those questions.

Not to create fear—but to restore proportion.

Nothing in this book argues against responsibility.

Responsibility matters.

But responsibility that endlessly defers gratification stops being stewardship and starts becoming absence.

And absence doesn't announce itself.

It accumulates.

Recognizing finitude doesn't solve anything.

It clarifies.

It brings the internal cost into focus.

And once that cost is seen, pretending there's unlimited time to compensate stops working.

That's not pressure.

That's reality.

This is the point where the book begins to close.

Not by offering answers—but by narrowing the field.

Because once time is recognized as finite, certain questions stop being theoretical.

They become personal.

And the most important one remains:

If time is limited, what am I actually spending mine **being present for**?

The book doesn't answer that.

It doesn't need to.

It only needed to make it visible.

Chapter 12 — This Book Stops Here

This isn't a call to quit.

It isn't a call to rebel.
It isn't a call to withdraw, opt out, or refuse participation.

Nothing in these pages asks you to abandon work, platforms, or responsibility.

That was never the point.

This book exists to **slow the moment before reaction**.

To pause the reflex to optimize, explain, fix, or perform.

Because most of what has been described here didn't happen through force.

It happened through speed.

When systems move quickly, people adapt quickly.

They don't stop to ask what something costs internally. They ask whether it works. Whether it moves. Whether it keeps things going.

That question has been running quietly in the background.

This book asked a different one.

Not: *What should I do?*
But: *What am I noticing while I do it?*

That difference matters.

INSIDER SIGNAL

You expect an answer here.
You don't receive one.

That pause is intentional.

Noticing is enough for now because noticing interrupts habit.

Habits operate automatically.
They rely on speed, repetition, and familiarity.

Attention slows them down.

Even briefly.

Most people assume clarity arrives as a conclusion.

A decision.
A plan.
A next step.

But clarity often arrives as **relief from urgency**.

As the quiet sense that something doesn't need to be solved immediately.

That you can sit with it.

Clarity doesn't rush because it doesn't need to.

Rushing belongs to systems that require constant output.

Clarity belongs to internal alignment—and alignment can't be forced.

It appears when interference drops.

INSIDER SIGNAL

You feel less compelled to act.
Not because you're stuck—
but because nothing is pressing you forward.

This book stops here because continuing would risk doing the thing it's been describing.

Offering solutions would create momentum.
Momentum would create performance.
Performance would create expectation.

Expectation would replace noticing.

You don't need another framework.

You don't need steps.

You don't need to agree with everything you read here.

You only need to notice when:

- You're present
- You're managing
- You're translating
- You're withholding

Those distinctions don't require action.

They require awareness.

Awareness changes things on its own.

Not dramatically.
Not all at once.

But steadily.

People often ask what comes next.

That question assumes sequence.

But what follows noticing isn't a step.

It's a **shift in orientation**.

Toward accuracy.
Toward restraint.
Toward internal contact.

This book doesn't claim that the world will slow down.

It won't.

It claims something simpler.

That you can.

INSIDER SIGNAL

You sense that something has loosened.
You can't name it.

You don't try to.

Stopping here is an act of respect.

For your autonomy.
For your timing.
For your capacity to discern without being led.

Nothing more needs to be said.

If something in these pages stayed with you, that's enough.

If it didn't, that's also fine.

This book wasn't written to convince.

It was written to **make a certain kind of noticing possible**.

What you do with that noticing isn't decided here.

It can't be.

And it shouldn't be.

This book stops here.

Not because there's nothing more to say—

But because saying more would get in the way of what just began.

The Marketplace of Selves is not a manifesto.
It is a mirror.

In a world where attention has become currency, and expression has become labor, most people adapt without ever noticing how they change. They shift how they speak, how they feel, and even how they think — all while believing nothing has altered.

This book doesn't offer formulas or solutions.
It offers something rarer: **visibility** — the ability to see what has shaped you before you agreed to it.

Here you have learned:

- How visibility systems guide performance without anyone saying so.
- Why metrics feel objective but act like pressure.
- How emotional range narrows without overt censorship.
- Why people rehearse for audiences that aren't there.
- And why clarity matters more than optimization.

This is a quiet invitation — not to quit, not to rebel, and not to fix everything.

But to notice.

And once you notice, everything looks different.

The Marketplace of Selves is the first step into the *LibertyTruth* series — a growing collection of books dedicated to clarity, discernment, and internal freedom. If you find yourself paying attention here, the journey continues — in other titles, on your terms, without urgency.

You don't have to agree.
You don't even have to act yet.
You only need to see.

About the Author

Trent Goodbaudy writes about clarity, perception, and the unseen pressures that shape modern life. His work focuses on how systems influence behavior quietly—often before people realize they've adapted.

He is the creator of the *LibertyTruth* series, an ongoing collection of observational books that examine identity, discernment, internal contact, and psychological restraint in an increasingly performative world. The series is not prescriptive and does not offer techniques or formulas. Each book isolates a different pressure and looks at what happens when it's seen clearly.

Some readers describe these books as quiet.
Others describe them as stabilizing.

The series continues to grow.

About LibertyTruth.org

Beyond books, LibertyTruth.org offers additional writing, tools, and projects for readers interested in sustained clarity rather than momentary insight. Nothing here promises transformation. Nothing claims to replace your judgment.

The goal is simpler—and harder.

To help you see what you may already be living inside, so that whatever choices follow are genuinely your own.

Visit **LibertyTruth.org** if you want to continue exploring this work—quietly, independently, and without instruction.

Made in the USA
Coppell, TX
22 February 2026

72089057R00059